Working Together to End Racism
Healing from the Damage Caused by Racism

Tim Jackins and others

A Publication of
United to End Racism

Reprinted October 2002

Copyright © 2002 by Rational Island Publishers. All rights reserved. No part of this pamphlet may be used or reproduced in any manner whatsoever without written permission except in the case of brief quotations embodied in critical articles or reviews.

For information write to:

*Rational Island Publishers
P.O. Box 2081, Main Office Station
Seattle, Washington 98111, U.S.A.*

ISBN: 1-58429-087-0
$2.00

CONTENTS

Foreword v
Introduction 1
The Damage Inflicted by Institutionalized Racism and
    Its Agents 7
A Second Form of Damage Caused by Racism:
    Internalized Racism 9
Healing from the Damage Inflicted by Racism and
    Internalized Racism 11
A Third Form of Damage Caused by Racism:
    The Effect of Racism on White People 15
White People as Allies to People Targeted by Racism 21
United to End Racism 25
The Basic Tool of United to End Racism: Re-evaluation
    Counseling 27
How to Begin "Re-evaluation Counseling" 31
Glossary 45

FOREWORD

United to End Racism (UER) is a collection of thousands of people of many racial groups in many countries. United to End Racism is a project of the Re-evaluation Counseling Communities, and the members of UER have learned and use the theory and tools of Re-evaluation Counseling. Re-evaluation Counseling (RC) has existed since the early 1950s. The RC Communities began the work of eliminating racism in the 1970s. In the late 1990s the RC Communities made the elimination of racism central to their work, and United to End Racism was created.

Our work is based on the belief that there is only one kind of human. We believe that skin color, gender, and so on, are minor differences between people. They are insignificant when considering the totality of the human being and the human mind. These differentiations have assumed irrational importance only because of their relationship to oppression. All forms of oppression make use of and exploit minor differences such as these. No group should ever be mistreated by other groups or by society as a whole. Oppression must end for every group.

This pamphlet is the collaborative effort of more than twenty people, people of many different racial groups. Its purpose is to convey what we have learned from our work to end racism. It does not attempt to describe the basic theory and practice of Re-evaluation Counseling, nor its application to individual struggles and to ending oppression. For this information, see the list at the back of this pamphlet or contact:

United to End Racism
A Project of the International
Re-evaluation Counseling Communities
719 Second Avenue North
Seattle, Washington 98109, USA
E-mail: ircc@rc.org
Tel. +1-206-284-0311
Fax +1-206-284-8429
Internet: <www.rc.org/uer>

INTRODUCTION

Groups of humans have been oppressed in a variety of ways throughout much of human history. Racism, one form of oppression, has existed for many centuries. Racism shapes and perpetuates the inequities of our societies and has become a part of our societal institutions.

Racism has become an integral part of our societies. It is not just an aberration of some small segment of the population. To end racism, policies must change, racist behavior must stop, the injustices from racism must be redressed, and all people must recover from the damage done to them by racism.

The main form of racism today is white racism—the one-way, institutionalized mistreatment of Africans, Indigenous peoples, Asians, Latin Americans, Arabs, and others and their descendants—people of color. Racism conditions people of European descent—white people—to act as agents of this mistreatment. All people are deeply hurt by racism. However, this system—of unequal access to the resources of society supported by violence, threats of violence, misinformation, lies, isolation, and greed—is directed at people targeted by racism and carried out by white people.

Again, one group is targeted by racist institutions and another is conditioned to act as the agent of racist oppression. This targeting has destroyed and damaged the lives of hundreds of millions of people, through slavery, apartheid, and racial discrimination in many forms. This conditioning has also deeply corrupted the lives of those who have been conditioned to act as agents of racism.

No group or individual should ever be targeted by racism. No characteristic, real or imagined, justifies racism. Those who have been targeted by racism comprise the vast majority of the human population. They are from a multitude of rich and vibrant cultures, cultures that have produced many of the best achievements of our species. There has never been, nor can there be, any rational justification of racism.

Although racism is aimed at particular sections of the population, it corrodes and corrupts the entire society, severely limiting society's progress. It also limits the progress of every individual in that society toward a full and meaningful life.

The work to end racist behavior undertaken by those who have been conditioned to be agents of racism is an important part of the work of United to End Racism. It is vital to the progress of all humans that those of us who have been conditioned by society to act as agents of racism make the ending of racism our goal. Racism has corrupted our lives, and it is in our interest, as well as in the interest of the rest of the world, that it be ended as quickly as possible.

The struggle to understand racism and to take action to eliminate it has progressed sufficiently that we can believe that racism will be ended in this century. People in many places have interrupted the worst manifestations of racism (such as slavery and apartheid) and have begun to secure broad agreement on policies to root out racism from many of society's institutions.

To end racism, it is vital that we remove racist policies from our institutions and ensure fair and just conditions of life for all. Accomplishing this will save future generations from the damage done to past generations. It is also vital to heal the damage done to individuals by racism. Healing this damage is not the same as ending racist policies. Only by healing the damage done to individuals can we be confident that racist attitudes and behaviors will not continue and that racist policies will not reappear in other guises.

To fully eliminate racism, we must heal three forms of damage.

The first form is the damage done to individuals targeted by racism—the hurts from being treated as inferior, denied basic material needs, denied a fair share of resources, demeaned, attacked, threatened with destruction, and much more. This damage is done to individuals through their contact with society's institutions and by the actions of other individuals.

The second form is the damage to members of targeted groups that occurs from having "internalized" racism. Racist attitudes can be so overpowering that they are absorbed by people targeted by racism. Racism shapes the way targeted people think and feel about themselves. It can make people mistreat themselves (and other members of their group) in ways that are similar to the mistreatment they have received from the agents of oppression. People end up mistreating themselves and each other. We call this "internalized" racism.

The third form of damage is the corruption of the minds and spirits of those conditioned by society to act as the agents of racism (i.e., white people). No one is born an agent of racism. No one is born with a racist attitude. Anyone with a racist attitude has first been mistreated and misinformed. He or she has been conditioned to play that role.

Although individuals of the oppressor group are accorded more rights and better material lives than people in the oppressed group, their lives and minds are corrupted by racism. Racism damages everyone. It is in no one's real human interest.

(Each of these forms of damage is described more fully in later sections of this pamphlet.)

All three forms of damage can be healed.

Even under the most severe racist oppression, people are able to move forward simply through the force of their own thinking and determination. However, unless they recover from the emotional hurts of racism, they continue to carry the effects of those hurts, and their thinking and behavior are affected by them. These hurts weigh heavily on each of them personally; the hurts also slow the work to bring about institutional change. Unhealed, these hurts from racism limit and damage everyone's abilities to think and work cooperatively and limit our capacity to end the other forms of oppression in our societies. They make the work and lives of those fighting institutionalized racism more difficult. In contrast, when people can heal from the effects of racism, they find it easier to work together, building strong alliances within their own liberation movement and between liberation movements.

If all racist behavior stopped immediately and racist policies were removed, the damage from past racism would not disappear. For those of us who are targeted, our feelings resulting from racism—feeling in danger, attacked, worthless, mistreated, ignored, doubting of ourselves—would continue to confuse us and erode our lives. For those of us trained by society to act as the agents of racism, the damage of having been conditioned to believe and act on the basis of racism (for example, feeling that one's own group is superior or feeling fear or discomfort around people targeted by racism) would also continue. It would confuse and corrupt both our thinking and behavior and lead to the re-enactment of racist policies and actions.

The work of United to End Racism is to remove the damage done to individuals by racism. Both for people targeted by racism and for white people, healing from racism involves releasing the emotional tensions left from early hurtful experiences in our lives. When we are allowed and encouraged to tell fully the stories of how racism has affected us, with others listening and giving their full attention, we will begin to heal. When we are able not only to recount the facts of these stories, but also to allow ourselves to feel and show what it was like for us personally—feel and express the rage, grief, or terror—we become increasingly free of the damage of racism. All the emotional effects of racism can be healed if the person is given enough time, attention, and understanding.

Healing from mistreatment is not easy work. Many of us resist it, even though without this healing, the rage, grief, and terror from the past continue to affect us. We may feel that we have been able to persist in life only by numbing ourselves and holding inside how we were hurt. It may seem unbearable to look at and feel those hurts again—perhaps because for so long most of us had no opportunity to tell our stories. Some of us believe that we are no longer hurting since we continued to function in our lives, often very well, after the incidents of mistreatment. We mistakenly believe that we "got over it." Or we unawarely accept the idea that it is impossible to heal fully from racism.

From our work in UER, we now know that it is possible for us to get completely free of the damage done by racism. We know that all of us are capable of freeing ourselves. We know that the apparently unbearable feelings do not persist once the healing process begins. And we find that once we begin healing from these hurts, we can think more clearly and act more powerfully in our work to end racism. Healing from the effects of racism is not a substitute for organizing and taking action against institutional racism, but we in UER have found it to be a vital component of the work to end racism.

In the following sections, the nature of the damage caused by racism and the process to heal from it are described in more detail.

THE DAMAGE INFLICTED BY INSTITUTIONALIZED RACISM AND ITS AGENTS

Institutionalized racism has spread world-wide, facilitated by colonialism, imperialism, and globalization. When one country takes over another country, subjugates its people, and extracts its resources, racism may be used to justify these actions. The enslavement of entire populations has been justified by portraying a group of people as less than human on the basis of their race. Race has been the excuse for the extermination and attempted extermination of whole populations—both openly, through violent acts, and more subtly, by taking away the natural resources on which they rely. In every form, racism aids and abets the expropriation of human labor and natural resources for the profit of a few. Racism has become a part of every society and each society's institutions.

For members of a target group, access to resources needed to survive and thrive—water, food, housing, education, jobs, medical and legal services, and so on—is severely limited by the operations of racism.

Societal institutions that are supposedly established to protect and inform their citizenry—for example, government agencies, the police, the criminal justice system, the media, educational institutions—often end up being agents of racism. People are targeted on the basis of race by these institutions in many ways: stereotyped as lawbreakers, as dangerous, as less intelligent, and so on. Schools portray a censored history of society, omitting the history of racism and the history of peoples targeted by racism. This distorts everyone's picture of the world and history. The tobacco, drug (legal and illegal), and alcohol industries make deliberate efforts to keep vulnerable people addicted to their products. They prey on people's feelings of hopelessness and powerlessness that result from racism.

Finally, white people, all of whom are conditioned to behave as agents of racism, wittingly or unwittingly act out racism daily. Members of targeted groups are threatened with bodily harm, injured, and killed. Slurs, epithets, and insults are frequent experiences. These overt racist behaviors are reinforced by the daily wear and tear of more subtle, but just as damaging, behaviors and attitudes. Members of targeted groups are demeaned, excluded, ignored, and generally treated with disrespect. A few of the many examples are: being ignored when trying to get service, being followed in stores, being harassed by police and subjected to racial profiling, being assumed to be troublemakers and dangerous criminals.

People targeted by racism are patronized and treated as less competent and less intelligent. These daily events serve to keep institutionalized racism in place. They are unavoidable reminders of how deep and widespread racism is in our society.

A SECOND FORM OF DAMAGE CAUSED BY RACISM: INTERNALIZED RACISM

Internalized racism occurs when people targeted by racism are, against their will, coerced and pressured to agree with the distortions of racism. Each of us targeted by racism fights, from childhood on, as long and as hard as we dare, to maintain a sense of ourselves as good, smart, strong, important, and powerful. However, in our societies, racist attitudes are so harsh, so pervasive, and so damaging that each of us is forced at times to turn racism in upon ourselves and seemingly agree with some of the conditioning, thereby internalizing the messages of racism. We come to mistreat ourselves and other members of our group in the same ways that we have been mistreated as the targets of racism.

Examples of internalized racism appear everywhere, for example:

• Racism has made us think of ourselves or each other as stupid, lazy, unimportant, or inferior.

• Racism has made us criticize or verbally attack each other, using the racist messages of our societies, or allow others in our group to do so.

• Racism has made us physically attack each other, playing out our rage about racism at one another.

• Racism has made us put our individual well-being last. Racism has made us unable to think about our physical and emotional health, making us vulnerable to heart disease, high blood pressure, obesity, diabetes, HIV/AIDS, ulcers, and more.

- Racism has made us criticize and beat our children in misguided efforts to "discipline" them and keep them from openly displaying pride or pleasure in themselves (attempting to make them less vulnerable to racism, but instead leaving them more beaten down and enraged).

- Racism has made us feel hopeless, despairing, and angry, which can make us vulnerable to the lure of alcohol and other drugs for "relief" from those feelings, even though we know that this does additional harm to ourselves and our families.

- Racism has made our various racial groups fight with each other over what seems like a scarcity of resources; racism has made our youth fight each other in gangs.

- Racism has made some of our group join racist institutions and take part in carrying out their racist policies against our own people.

- Racism has made us feel disconnected from other members of our group, or made us divide or categorize each other by behaviors or lifestyles, believing that some of us are "better" or "more legitimate" than others and that what some others do is "not part of" our cultures.

- Racism has made us place higher value on members of our group who appear more white, and denigrate those who have darker skin, kinkier hair, or other "less white" features. We also do the reverse—we target those with lighter skins as not being "black enough," not legitimate persons of color.

We are not to blame for any of these attitudes or behaviors, but we can increasingly understand them and take steps to end them and to heal the damage done to us by this form of racism.

HEALING FROM THE DAMAGE INFLICTED BY RACISM AND INTERNALIZED RACISM

To heal from the damage inflicted by racism and internalized racism, we need to tell our stories—how racism has affected our lives, what has happened to us and to our people. We need the chance to openly express our feelings about our experiences of racism. When we do this, the damage done by racism begins to dissipate. We start seeing ourselves more clearly as good, smart, strong, complete human beings. We feel and act more powerfully and hopeful about ending racism and other oppressions. We treat each other more respectfully and cooperatively.

For this healing process to work well, we need someone to listen attentively to our stories—someone who is sincerely interested and who stays relaxed while we express our emotions. We need someone who encourages us to tell the full story of what happened and how we felt and to use the process of emotional release—allowing ourselves to cry, laugh, or rage. Any two individuals can agree to take turns listening to each other, without interruption, for a specified amount of time (for example, half an hour each), encouraging each other to share their experiences fully and not hold back their emotions.

United to End Racism has found that safety for healing from internalized racism builds when people meet not only in pairs but also in support groups with others from a similar background or heritage (for example, African or Indigenous). In these support groups each member has an equal amount of uninterrupted time to share experiences of racism while the others listen attentively. The support group leader encourages the person talking to express his or her thoughts and feelings. The leader welcomes and encourages the tears, trembling, raging, and laughter that often occur spontaneously as people talk about their struggles with racism.

When we first participate in these groups, internalized racism may cause negative feelings about each other (distrust, dislike, upset, and so on) to surface. These feelings arise from internalized racism and will disappear as people tell their stories and hear others' stories. In the meantime, members of the group need to make an agreement to not act on the basis of such feelings.

Questions such as the following can help members of support groups begin to identify and focus on internalized racism:

• What information about yourself would you like others to know—about your heritage, country of origin, family, class background, and so on?

• What makes you proud about being a member of this group (e.g., being of African descent), and what do you love about other members of this group?

• What has been hard about being a member of this group, and what do you sometimes not like about others in this group?

• What were your early life experiences with people in this group? How were you treated? How did you feel about others in your group when you were young?

When people are given a chance to talk and express their feelings, internalized racism is directly challenged. As emotions are released, people's negative feelings about themselves and others in their groups begin to disappear. People are able to think more clearly. They can reach for cooperative relationships more easily. Once groups of people have had a chance to meet separately in this way, greater unity and participation are possible when they join with larger, more diverse groups of people.

Support groups can be used in many settings—at the workplace, at school, in religious settings, in the neighborhood. Support groups are increasingly helpful for the participants over time. As the participants get to know each other, they become closer to each other, more supportive of each other, and more open. Even two people can have a support group, taking turns listening to one another. Support groups can also be used for non-race-based groups—such as women, young people, and working-class people.

(See page 31, "How to Begin 'Re-evaluation Counseling,'" for information on creating opportunities for people to listen to one another and heal from the damage done by racism.)

A THIRD FORM OF DAMAGE CAUSED BY RACISM: THE EFFECT OF RACISM ON WHITE PEOPLE

Some of us have not been the targets of racism. Instead, we have been conditioned by society to act out the oppressor role of racism. Because we have not been the targets of racism, we have not suffered the damage described above. However, in a different way, racism greatly damages our minds and lives as white people.

HOW WHITE RACISM IS INSTALLED

Racism is contrary to the fundamental nature of every human being. All human beings begin life caring deeply about all other human beings. Until we ourselves are hurt—put down, ignored, threatened, scared, beaten, criticized, isolated, and so on—each of us wants all people to be treated well. None of us, including white people, would ever participate in the racist mistreatment or oppression of other humans unless we had first been hurt. However, once hurt, we are vulnerable to hurting others—by participating in oppressive systems and acting oppressively as individuals.

In an oppressive society, few people escape being hurt in ways that make us feel scared and bad about ourselves. It is when we are scared and when we feel bad about ourselves that we are most vulnerable to believing racist messages.

In a racist culture there is a constant barrage of racist messages and practices—from family, friends, acquaintances, schools, the media, and many other institutions.

No one can grow up in such an environment and escape its effects. In this way the society installs racism on every white person. It does so regardless of how strongly or for how long we actively resist.

Racism is instilled in white children at a very young age, often by the adults children most love and depend on. Children are conditioned to be racist by repeatedly hearing negative comments about targeted groups, by witnessing mistreatment or violence turned on those groups, and by being told that people of targeted groups are less valuable. In some cases, adults pass racism on to young people by threatening violence or disapproval. Because white people are often kept isolated from people targeted by racism, false stereotypes can go unquestioned. The indoctrination of racism begins when we are very young and is fostered by the relative powerlessness of children in most societies.

WHITE PEOPLE ACT AS AGENTS OF RACISM

As a result of these hurts, all white people have been conditioned to accept as true, at some level, the lies of racism and to carry racist feelings. Some white people stop questioning these feelings and act out these "beliefs" in hateful and oppressive ways. Other white people intellectually reject the content of racist messages and try to treat people targeted by racism respectfully and as equals. But even though we may act with goodwill toward people targeted by racism or actively engage in fighting racism, still negative attitudes (unjustified fears, the seeking of approval, feelings of superiority, and so on) surface from time to time, attitudes that must be battled in order for us to act consistently according to our best thinking. In addition, feelings of sadness, guilt, shame, and hopelessness about racism interfere with our ability to act effectively against racism and to make and maintain deep friendships with persons targeted by racism.

It is when we feel scared, mistreated, or bad about ourselves that we have the most difficulty in acting on our thinking instead of our upsets and fears. Those are the times when white people are most pulled to act on the basis of the racism we've heard and seen, sometimes acting it out subtly and unawarely and other times overtly and harshly.

WHITE RACISM ALSO HURTS WHITE PEOPLE

Racism greatly damages the lives of people targeted by it. Racism also hurts white people deeply. (This is true of any group that acts out oppression.) It compounds the ways those of us who are white already feel bad about ourselves. Not standing up against racism erodes our integrity and undermines our sense of goodness and self-worth.

White people become separated from the majority of the world's people, know little about them, and miss close involvement in the lives of a rich variety of people. We numb ourselves to the pain caused to others by racism, and, in doing so, we become less able to care about any people.

Racism also erodes relationships between white people—we do not want to be associated with "that white racist" or "that white liberal." When we feel confused about our own goodness and worth, it can be difficult for us to appreciate the goodness and worth of other white people.

Many white people feel a responsibility to undo the damage done by white people historically, and we may even take action to do so. However, we still carry feelings of guilt, hopelessness, and powerlessness about actually eliminating racism and creating a just and equitable society.

WHITE PEOPLE HEALING FROM THE HURTS OF WHITE RACISM

United to End Racism and Re-evaluation Counseling (see pages 27 to 44 for more information on Re-evaluation Counseling) have valuable experience and tools for white people to use in ending racism. We have learned that any and all "oppressor roles" are installed by hurting people very deeply. White people's oppressive behavior arises from deep emotional damage. Sustained emotional work is required for us to free ourselves from racism. To create a just society, white people must not only inform ourselves fully about racism and take action to end it, but we must also heal from the damage caused by being exposed to racism and by having participated in it.

To do this emotional work, white people can take turns listening to each other in pairs and in groups. We need to remember and tell our stories having to do with racism and assist one another to release the intense feelings that underlie our stories—by crying, laughing, trembling, and raging.

Some specific ways white people can work to heal ourselves from white racism follow. With another white person listening to us and encouraging us to be open, we can talk and express our feelings about ourselves fully (showing all the feelings we have) about:

- our early experiences with people targeted by racism;
- the lies we were told about groups targeted by racism;
- the attitudes that were held by people around us;
- the times we unthinkingly acted out the racism that had been installed on us;

- our efforts to have good relationships with people from targeted groups;
- how we have fought against racism;
- what discouraged us from believing that we could end racism;
- the many good acts against racism by white people.

To do this work, those of us who are white need settings in which we can be open about racism without being blamed or shamed, where we know we are cared about and respected. Blame and shame interfere with freeing white people of racism and actually serve to hold racist attitudes and behavior in place. Listening pairs and support groups must be safe places where we are not criticized for our feelings or past actions. Under these conditions, we can remember and tell what happened to us and what we did with regard to racism and release the painful emotions from these experiences.

Those of us who are white also need to listen to people targeted by racism and learn, first-hand, what racism has been like for them. Then we, in turn, need to be listened to by another white person in order to release the feelings that surface when we hear these stories. People targeted by racism should not be expected to participate in pairs or groups where white people are working on their own racism; white people need to learn to do this work with one another and become allies to each other in ending racism. It is the job of white people, not the job of people targeted by racism, to do the work to both stop white people from perpetuating racism and to help those targeted by racism heal the damage they carry.

With emotional release, white people are able to think freshly about our experiences. We clear our minds of the lies and misinformation. We get better at making friendships with people targeted by racism and at deepening those relationships. We are better able to appreciate the cultures and achievements of people targeted by racism. We also deepen our ability to appreciate the cultures and achievements of other white people and our ability to build strong relationships with each other.

We become partners with people targeted by racism in their efforts to heal from having lived in a racist society. We begin taking effective steps to end racism as we free ourselves of the effects of racism, all of which improves our lives in countless ways.

(See page 31, "How to Begin 'Re-evaluation Counseling,'" for information on creating opportunities for people to listen to one another and heal from the damage done by racism.)

WHITE PEOPLE AS ALLIES TO PEOPLE TARGETED BY RACISM

An important part of ending racism and all other oppressions is to develop alliances between those targeted by the oppression and those outside the targeted group. Eliminating racism requires the development of strong alliances among groups of people targeted by racism and also with white people who are committed to ending racism. These white allies are people who have decided to work for the liberation of all people targeted by racism. White people in this ally role work alongside groups of people targeted by racism and demonstrate by their actions and words that they support the goals and visions of those groups. In United to End Racism, we have learned a great deal about building alliances and about white people becoming effective allies.

STEPS TOWARD BECOMING WHITE ALLIES

Being a white ally means taking visible stands against all forms of racism. White allies engage in campaigns for the elimination of racism by backing anti-racism organizations that are led by people targeted by racism. We do so without taking over or imposing our own ideas. Neither do we expect people targeted by racism to do most of the work. We stand with them and intervene when racist attacks come their way. We independently stand against racism whenever and wherever it occurs.

Being a white ally means working on, and eliminating, our own racism and working to heal the places our hurts make us silent and passive about racism.

White allies stand firmly against any playing out of internalized racism. That is, when people targeted by racism are in the grips of self-doubt, feeling bad about themselves, or having conflicts with one another, white allies can remind them that they are good, smart, and capable, that their relationships with each other are important, and that the negative feelings they have about each other are usually a result of having internalized the messages of racism.

Being a white ally means learning correct information about the lives and histories of groups targeted by racism. On a daily basis, white people are fed lies, half-truths, stereotypes, and incorrect notions about people targeted by racism, about ourselves as white people, and about relationships between white people and people targeted by racism. For institutionalized racism to continue, oppressive societies would have to keep white people confused, uncertain, fearful, and insecure, with these feelings often covered with a layer of arrogance and false confidence. Being an ally means healing the places where we have been unaware and uninformed. It means actively seeking correct information.

Being a white ally means working toward long-term friendships with people targeted by racism. Every person naturally and inherently wants to end the oppression of every other person, particularly people they care about. Only the racism with which white people are conditioned keeps us from such caring—and from standing up against oppression. The messages of separation, difference, isolation, and fear that underpin racism are interrupted and refuted as white people move toward relationships with people targeted by racism.

Being a white ally means training and building around us a group of white allies who are committed to eliminating racism. This work involves assisting other white people to heal from the racist patterns of behavior they have been forced to take on. It involves not giving up on other white people and working to build friendships with them, whether or not they "act racist."

White allies can help people targeted by racism heal from the racist hurts they have suffered by providing places where they can tell their stories and fully express their grief or anger or fear. The basic requirements for this healing are: (1) being listened to without interruption, (2) being encouraged to share their experiences of racism fully, and (3) being encouraged to openly express their feelings about these experiences.

As we white people take on ending racism and being allies to people targeted by racism, we need to understand that this is for our own benefit as well as others. Racism gives us, as white people, a distorted picture of the world and thereby distorts our lives. It erodes our humanity. Ending racism means getting a fuller picture of the world and reality. Ending racism means recovering from the dehumanizing damage that racism has done to us—reclaiming our courage, integrity, sense of self-worth, and our full humanity. Finally, ending racism means having a world that is right for everyone, a world where everyone matters.

UNITED TO END RACISM

United to End Racism (UER) is a group of people of many racial groups and all ages and backgrounds, in many different countries, who are dedicated to eliminating racism in the world. We understand that eliminating racism is necessary for humankind to progress. We are committed to ending racism, and we support the efforts of other groups to accomplish this goal.

The main work of UER is to illuminate the damage done to individuals by racism and to undo this damage on an individual basis, using the resources and process of Re-evaluation Counseling. As people do this work, they become better able:

- to interrupt racism in their daily lives;
- to free themselves from all of racism's effects;
- to take leadership;
- to form deep relationships across racial lines;
- to remove racism from our societies' institutions; and
- to support the work of other individuals and organizations in ending racism.

United to End Racism also examines the racism in our societies' institutions and encourages its members to both become actively aware of it and to find new ways of combatting and eliminating it. United to End Racism offers both an ongoing system of support that assists people to sustain their efforts to eliminate racism, and effective tools for eliminating racism in individuals. These tools can be taught and used on a one-to-one basis and with groups.

Through its work, UER has developed a new and important understanding of racism and the relationships between racism and other oppressions. This understanding includes how racism and other oppressions are inflicted upon people, how they damage people, how this damage is passed from generation to generation, how people can resist such damage, and how people can recover from it. Our understanding is that racism is unintentionally internalized by those who have been targeted by it. It then operates within the targeted group to make that group's work to end racism more difficult. United to End Racism has also developed an understanding of the effects of racism on members of oppressor groups and how racist attitudes are installed on and persist in them.

Using this understanding of racism, UER has developed methods for undoing its damage. The work to recover from the damage of racism is done, in different ways, both by people who are members of groups targeted by racism and by people who are members of groups that play oppressive, racist roles.

THE BASIC TOOL OF UNITED TO END RACISM: RE-EVALUATION COUNSELING

Re-evaluation Counseling is a process for freeing humans and society as a whole from the damage done by racism, other oppressions, and the hurts that come from other sources so that we may resume fully-intelligent functioning. Re-evaluation Counseling is practiced in pairs, by people listening to each other and assisting each other to tell their full stories of being hurt, including the grief, rage, or fear involved. Because no money is exchanged between people who counsel one another in these pairs, Re-evaluation Counseling can be used by any individual, regardless of his or her economic circumstances.

Members of the Re-evaluation Counseling Communities have worked on eliminating racism since the 1970s. In 1999 the International Re-evaluation Counseling Communities designated eliminating racism as our key issue, accelerating work on eliminating this oppression. Within the RC Communities people attend caucuses and workshops in which we exchange counseling to free ourselves from the effects of racism. Some of these caucuses and workshops are for people of various heritages. Some are for single-heritage groups (African descendants, Indigenous peoples, and so on).

Re-evaluation Counseling (also known as RC or Co-Counseling) views all human beings as inherently intelligent, cooperative, and good. We assume it is natural for a human to have good relations with all other humans, to think well, to act wisely and successfully, and to enjoy life.

In this view, every human being acts and cooperates well except where "memories" of past distress interfere. Then irrational behavior, negative feelings, and failure to cooperate or communicate replace the inherent human behavior. These "distress patterns" of behavior are the residue of physical or emotional hurts, many of them dating back to childhood, from which we have never fully recovered. They affect us when something in the current environment reminds us of the earlier times of distress.

The residual effects of past distress experiences could have been thrown off quickly and permanently, at the time we were hurt, through the natural channels of emotional discharge (for example, crying, laughing, and trembling). After emotional discharge, a person's mind is able to think more clearly and re-evaluate what happened in the distressing incident.

Instead, some of the social conditioning against emotional discharge carried by our cultures and rigidly inflicted upon us when we were children ("Don't cry," "Be a big boy," and so on) has interfered with, and prevented, recovery from our hurts, leading to an increasing accumulation of distresses and tensions. By the time we are adults, this has severely limited our original abilities to achieve good relationships with others, to succeed, and to enjoy life. It also interferes with our collective progress towards a society that supports all people to thrive in cooperative, respectful relationships.

In Re-evaluation Counseling we regain the natural ability to heal from hurt. The prime requirement for this is a listener (the "counselor") who is sincerely interested, who will remain relaxed in the face of our tensions, and who understands how the process of emotional discharge operates.

Many of our accumulated distresses result from societally-imposed hurts that we call oppression (racism is one example). Every adult in every present society has been conditioned, through the imposition of distress patterns, into functioning in both oppressed and oppressor roles. (For example, the same person can both be oppressed by racism and act in the oppressor role with regard to sexism.)

Oppression is neither inevitable nor inherent in human beings. It arises and operates only on the basis of distress patterns. No human being would agree to submit to oppression unless a distress pattern of such submission had been previously installed while the human being was hurting. No human being would ever agree to, or participate in, oppressing another human being unless a distress pattern had been previously installed. Once these patterns are in place, we are susceptible to acting irrationally and oppressively toward others, including people in our own group, and even toward ourselves. (For example, when racism has hurt people to the point where they unknowingly internalize it, they may demean and mistreat themselves and their own people.)

Individuals can be freed from the damage caused by racism, and other oppressions, through the processes of emotional discharge. This healing empowers individuals to engage in the organizing and struggle necessary for the elimination of racism from institutions and society.

Re-evaluation Counseling is currently practiced in ninety-three countries. More information about Re-evaluation Counseling may be found on our web site at: <http://www.rc.org>.

HOW TO BEGIN
"RE-EVALUATION COUNSELING"

If you wish to try Re-evaluation Counseling (RC or Co-Counseling) for yourself, the following will help you get started.

In its basic form, the practice of Co-Counseling simply consists of two people taking turns listening to each other. It's like a conversation in some ways, but it's different, too. It's a more careful, effective kind of listening. It is about listening and paying attention to what you hear. It is thinking about the person who is saying it, and thinking about what he or she is saying, without interrupting the listening by offering suggestions or comments, but simply listening wholeheartedly.

TAKE TURNS LISTENING

It's simple to get started. It just takes two people. Find a friend (or co-worker or spouse) who will try it with you. Agree that you will take turns listening to each other without interruption for an equal amount of time, and agree how long that time will be. Then decide who is going to talk first. That person then talks about whatever he or she wants to talk about. The listener simply pays attention, tries to understand fully, and doesn't interrupt to give advice or comment or tell how he or she feels about what is said.

After the agreed-upon time, the talker becomes the listener, and the one who listened first now talks about anything he or she wants to talk about.

It's a fair exchange. Neither person owes anything to the other. Afterwards, both people usually feel refreshed and think more easily.

It is important to agree that whatever is said by either person will not be repeated by the listener outside of the session. This makes it safe to talk more fully.

These exchanges are good to do whenever you get a chance. As you listen this way more times, you get to know each other better and like each other more and more.

You also get better at listening. The whole process becomes more effective the more times you use it.

Co-Counseling "turns" or "sessions" can be as long or as short as you have time for. Even a few minutes shared with your Co-Counselor can make a big difference in how you are able to think and function, and two hours shared is much better.

GETTING ONE'S FEELINGS "OUT"

Sometimes the person talking (the "talker" or the "client") may begin to laugh or cry or speak loudly, or sometimes tremble or yawn. While this display of emotion may initially make you uncomfortable, it is actually a sign of progress. It simply means that the person is tense about something, perhaps feeling some embarrassment or grief or fear or physical discomfort, and she or he is releasing the tension. She or he is becoming "un-embarrassed," "un-sad," "un-afraid." We sometimes call the release of tension in these ways "discharge." The person listening (the "counselor") can feel pleased if this happens and should continue to pay attention to the client without trying to stop any discharge that is occurring. If the client stops his or her own discharge, the listener can reassure him or her that it is fine to continue.

WHAT DO YOU THINK ABOUT THIS?

This is the basic idea of Co-Counseling—two people take turns listening to each other. You can make many changes in your life just by knowing and doing this.

If you're reading this with someone, you might want to stop reading at this point and try listening to each other, ten minutes for each person. Afterwards, tell each other what your impression was.

Once you have "Co-Counseled" a few times with the same person, take time to talk it over and see what you each think of the experience. How did you like having someone listen to you without interrupting? Did you enjoy it? How did you like listening without interrupting? Would you like to continue trying this? You can read further in this pamphlet for more information about how to do this well.

TO BE AN EFFECTIVE COUNSELOR

Respect your client and the importance of your listening. Assume that your client is intelligent, powerful, and loving. Communicate your confidence in him or her. People have been hurt many times in their lives and it is these hurts that interfere with people's ability to think, learn, love, and act on their own thinking. Give your client your best attention. Assume that your listening and caring will make a difference. Remember that you need not try to "make something happen." The healing process is natural, part of the way a human mind functions. Instead, your job is to create a favorable situation for the client to use in the best way he or she can determine.

Listen with expectation and delight. Think of the alive interest you would like to see in someone listening to you. Your client would like something similar. As you pay attention, you can figure out exactly what encourages this client to talk as fully and freely as possible.

Pay attention to your client's concerns, not your own. Keep your memories of your own similar experiences and emotional reactions to yourself. You have agreed to listen to the client during his or her turn. You can examine your reactions during your own turn. If you find it disturbing when your client cries, laughs, or trembles, save those feelings for your own session. In this way you can recover your ability to listen easily.

Put your attention on whatever your client wants to talk about. As people talk to an interested listener, they reveal more about themselves and their experiences. Talking about a current problem will often lead to talking about events in the past—unhealed hurts that have been with the person for a long time and are at the root of current upsets. If your client is focused on an issue, just listen. Simple, interested listening will build the trust that will eventually allow your client to release the painful emotion he or she carries. If your client quickly moves on from a topic you think might be significant, you may invite and encourage returning to that topic. Although the client is in charge of the Co-Counseling session and will exercise his or her judgment on what issues are important and safe enough to address, your encouragement may be needed for the client to be able to stay with a difficult but important topic.

Help your client focus on the hurt by asking simple questions about it. Try not to analyze or "psychologize." It is the client's talking about the hurt that will bring their own fresh understanding and the release of painful emotion. Do not try to think for your client. His or her difficulties in handling the problems, challenges, oppressions, and hurtful experiences of the present are often the result of past situations that left a residue of confusing feelings. You can occasionally ask your client how present difficulties remind him or her of earlier hurts.

Assist your client to fully express the painful feelings he or she talks about. Human beings can shed feelings of upset and the rigid reactions that go with them. Your listening and attitude of caring, respect, attention, hope, delight, and confidence will allow your client to trust you and will powerfully contradict the impressions left by the hurtful experiences in his or her life. With that contradiction, your client will begin to cry, tremble, perspire, laugh, or rage. When this emotional release begins, your role is to help it continue by listening and by helping the client to repeat the thought, words, or gestures that brought on the release. Certain actions may make it safer for the release of the client's feelings. Holding hands may help your client to cry harder. You can see what allows your client to release his or her feelings more fully.

In general, people will release emotions when they feel safe and respected, when the release process is encouraged, when the counselor shows that he or she has seen the client's distresses (as well as the client's goodness), and when the client can tell that the feelings left by the hurts are not the reality about him or her, or the world.

WHAT TO DO IN A SESSION

Time spent listening to each other without interruption is often called a "session." Below are some things that you can experiment with doing in your sessions.

"News and Goods"

You can start your session as client by telling your counselor about good things, big or small, that have happened lately. It could be the beautiful sunset you saw last night, or your new job, or a problem you figured out last week. The idea is to give yourself a chance to notice the things that are going well. (This is especially a good idea if you feel discouraged. It helps remind you that maybe things aren't as bad as they feel.) Sometimes people spend whole Co-Counseling sessions just telling "news and goods" and leave feeling much more positive and thinking more clearly.

Recent Upsets

If something has happened recently that you are upset about, a Co-Counseling session is a good place to talk about it. You can tell as much or as little about it as you would like, and you can tell it once or you can tell it over and over. You will probably find that lots of your problems seem to get much smaller if you just get a chance to talk about them without someone trying to give you advice or solve them for you. You will find, more often than not, that you can think of a good solution if you just have someone hear you out and show confidence in you while you feel upset and talk about the problem.

Troubles from the Past

If you use your turn as client to talk about something that is bothering you, you can sometimes, after you have had a chance to talk about the upset for a while, ask yourself (or your counselor can ask you), "What does this situation or this feeling remind you of? When have you felt like this before?" You will almost always think of some situation from the past that was hurtful or upsetting in a similar way. It will be plain that old feelings from that time are still lingering in your mind, adding more confusion and feelings to the present situation than there would otherwise be. If you can talk about the earlier situation, what happened then, how you felt, and how it affected you, some of those old feelings can then be discharged, leaving you with a fresher look at the present difficulty.

Life Stories

If you come to your session as client and there seems to be nothing in your present life that you need to talk about, try telling your life story. Most people have never had a chance to tell the whole story of their life, and everyone needs a chance to do this. As you tell the story of your life, certain incidents will seem more important in their effect on you, good or bad, than others. These incidents are worth coming back to and talking about many times in Co-Counseling sessions. Getting a chance to review them over and over, with someone who is really listening, can make a surprising difference in your thinking. Bad feelings left over from old, hurtful experiences (including experiences that you thought were "behind you") can come to the surface and discharge, leaving you with a lighter step and freer thoughts. Good experiences, when reviewed with the attention of a good listener, can also help bad feelings from old, difficult times to discharge, and this can help you regain a positive outlook.

Self-Appreciation

Most of us have been belittled or mistreated enough that it is now difficult for us to feel good about ourselves. We have been "blamed" for things when we were doing our best. We have been told many untrue things. We have been told that if we like ourselves, we are "conceited" and that we shouldn't feel good about ourselves. This isn't true. People deserve and need to feel good about themselves. When we do feel good about ourselves, we treat other people better, not worse.

When it is your turn as a client in a session, tell your counselor what you like about yourself. Tell this to him or her in a tone of voice that sounds like you are proud of yourself (not "superior," just proud). Tell your counselor this over and over. You may find it difficult, but stick with it. Don't stop yourself from laughing or crying or any other type of discharge. Try to appreciate everything about yourself. When you notice which things feel harder to appreciate (for example, how you look or how smart you are), focus on appreciating those things. You will probably remember incidents from your life of being criticized, blamed, or mistreated. These incidents will be good to look at and talk about in this or another session.

Goals

It helps your life go better to set goals for yourself or review your progress towards goals that you have already set. This is a useful thing to do when you are client in a Co-Counseling session. Talk through the different periods of your life, tentatively deciding what you want to accomplish tomorrow, next week, this year, in the next five years, in the next twenty years, in your lifetime. As you talk about each future period, you can think through the steps that you will need to take to reach these goals.

Occasionally reviewing your goals and any apparent obstacles will tend to assist you in achieving them.

LETTING DISCHARGE CONTINUE

If you talk about something as client that results in lively talking, laughter, tears, shaking, sweating, or yawning (all forms of discharge), don't rush on to something else. Try repeating what you were saying or doing several times until you are no longer discharging. It's worth doing this over and over for as much time as you can take. The greatest benefits of Co-Counseling come after these releases of tension. They make it possible to think and act in ways that have been inhibited before.

ENDING A SESSION

At the end of a Co-Counseling session, especially if you've been talking about something difficult for you, take a few moments to re-direct your thoughts to something you are looking forward to, or to some simple subject you don't feel tense about, for example, the names of some friends or some favorite foods, or some scenery that you enjoy looking at. This helps make a relaxed change from being a client to becoming a counselor if it is your turn to do this, or to going on to other activities.

HELPING YOUR SESSIONS GO WELL

• Confidentiality

For each person to feel safe to talk about whatever he or she needs to, it is important to agree that you won't discuss the contents of the session with anyone later. Keep whatever is said in the session completely confidential.

• Keep Your Relationship Clear

This relationship will not work well if you try to develop other relationships together. Keep the relationship, purely and simply, as a Co-Counseling relationship. This will free you from having conflicting expectations of each other. You will be better able to put your full and single-minded support to your partner's development and growth.

• Drugs and Alcohol

Keep in mind that alcohol and drugs interfere with the good effects of being listened to in this way.

• Keeping a Longer View

The longer view is that you are forming a very special long-term relationship. The two of you get to share your minds to a very full extent and do it indefinitely. You will be helping and supporting each other to have big and full lives. Over time, you will witness exciting changes in your partner. He or she will reclaim the parts of his or her life taken away by hurtful experiences of the past.

SUPPORT GROUPS

It also works well to get a small group of people together to take turns listening to each other. (In RC we call this a "support group.") Each person gets an equal amount of time to talk while the rest of the group listens.

One person acts as the leader of the group to help the group decide how much time each person will get, who will go first, and so on. When each person has had his or her turn as client, you can end the group meeting with each person getting a chance to say what he or she liked best about being in the group meeting or something he or she is looking forward to.

Each "client" should have a "counselor"—a group member actively supporting him or her to speak and encouraging the release of painful emotions. A designated leader can act as counselor for each person in the group, or each person can choose his or her own counselor. The group should also choose an overall leader whose job is to ensure that the group functions well.

Support groups can meet as often or as many times as the group members wish. The group can be a group of friends, co-workers, neighbors, or people with a similar background or interest. Sharing something in common with the group often helps people feel safer to talk about things they need to talk about. For example, there have been support groups of women, men, African descendant people, Asians, Indigenous people, Arabs, Chicanos/as, parents, young people, working-class people, people of a certain religion, disabled people, artists, and many others.

About eight people seems to be the optimum size for a group, but they can function well both smaller and larger. If the group becomes too large, it can be divided and a second group formed with a new leader chosen for the new group. Inviting friends to the group is a good way to introduce more people to Co-Counseling.

Support groups are a good structure for people from a similar background to use to talk about what they like about being from that background and what they are proud of about the people from that background.

Support groups are also good for talking about what has been hard about having that particular background, what they wish people understood about it, and what hopes and dreams they have for people from their group. For example, in a support group for people of African descent, each person would have a turn sharing what he or she likes about being of African descent, what has been hard about being of African descent, what he or she would like other groups to understand about people of African descent, how he or she would like to see the lives of people of African descent improve, and what ways he or she would like to reach out to other people of African descent.

All the members of the group listen respectfully, without interrupting the client. With uninterrupted listening and with encouragement from the group, the client will be able to express feelings of upset associated with distressing experiences in his or her past. Being in the center of a group of people who openly show their support counters the hurtful messages of racism and other oppressions. With this active support, the client will talk and will often begin to cry, tremble, laugh, or express fury on their way to recovering from the hurts of racism. As in a session, confidentiality is important, and support group members need to commit themselves to keeping what is said in the group confidential.

People targeted by racism can release painful emotions if listened to with respect while they talk about the details of their mistreatment. It is also important that they express pride in who they are and the groups they belong to, and the fact that they have endured the oppression and managed to flourish in spite of it.*

IF YOU WANT TO LEARN MORE

If you try Co-Counseling and you'd like to learn more, you can get in touch with the main Re-evaluation Counseling office (look at the end of this pamphlet before the Glossary for the address and phone number), and ask if there are any Co-Counselors who live near you. You could also order a few introductory publications. Some good readings to start with are:

• *The Human Side of Human Beings* (the theory of RC), $4.00 (US)

• *The Fundamentals of Co-Counseling Manual* (the beginning practice of RC), $6.00 (US)

• *The Art of Listening* (an introductory talk about RC), $2.00 (US)

• *An Introduction to Co-Counseling* (a very short description of RC), $1.00 (US)

---

* White allies will also find support groups useful for discharging the hurts they have experienced from racism (isolation, loss of relationships, confusion) and on the oppressor roles into which they have been conditioned. Group members need to maintain the attitude that each white person is completely good and not at fault for his or her racist conditioning. This will help the client release the hurts that have led to his or her oppressive behavior.

• *The Human Situation* (essays on different topics), $6.00 (US)

• *Present Time* (a general journal published four times a year), $3.50 (US)

We have literature published in about thirty different languages, written by Co-Counselors from all over the world, with stories about using RC and with information about people of different ages, backgrounds, and situations.

Videotapes and audiotapes are also available. Almost all are in English, but we do have different video formats for different countries as well as typed transcripts for each videotape. Someone at the main office can tell you which ones might be good for you to start with.

If you can't afford to pay for literature, explain this and ask if it is possible for Outreach Funds to pay for some literature in order for you to get started.

If you are very interested in learning more about RC, are ready to commit some time to learning it, and know other people who are eager to learn, we may be able to have a teacher make a visit to your group or bring one of you to a workshop.

There is an RC web site on the Internet, <http://www.rc.org/>, with information and many articles. If you are in an area which does not yet offer RC classes but you can connect to the Internet, you might find the on-line "class" helpful.

People who use Re-evaluation Counseling find that it helps them think better, improve relationships, have fuller lives, and enjoy life more. Co-Counselors' lives improve as they use RC, and they get better at using it. They often teach other people about RC and teach them how to teach other people, so that in some places there are many people using RC, holding classes and workshops, learning from each other, and supporting and encouraging each other.

There are also a few ground rules and a set of "Community Guidelines," which help Co-Counselors keep things clear and well organized.

We welcome your interest and participation in Re-evaluation Counseling and look forward to hearing from you.

United to End Racism
A Project of the International
Re-evaluation Counseling Communities
719 Second Avenue North
Seattle, Washington 98109, USA
E-mail: ircc@rc.org
Tel. +1-206-284-0311
Fax +1-206-284-8429
Internet: <www.rc.org/uer>

GLOSSARY

Agents of racism — those conditioned to carry out racism, for example, people of European heritage or white people.

Client — in the Co-Counseling session, the person who is being listened to, and is encouraged to talk and to release emotions.

Co-Counseling — the practice of Re-evaluation Counseling.

Counselor — in the Co-Counseling session, the person who listens and encourages emotional release by the client.

Distress pattern or pattern of behavior — a rigid set of "thoughts," behaviors, and feelings left by an unhealed hurtful experience or experiences.

Emotional discharge — a process inherent to human beings that heals the emotional damage from distressful incidents. Outward signs of this process include animated talking, crying, trembling, expressions of anger, and laughter.

Intelligence — as used here, the ability to create a new, creative response to fit each new, present situation. Unhealed distress experiences slow down and reduce this ability.

Internalized racism — the false and hurtful attitudes of invalidation about oneself or one's group; these attitudes were originally imposed by racism from the outside, but the targeted person has "taken them to heart" and believes them (until these attitudes can be healed).

Liberation movement — the program and process of freeing one's self and one's group from oppression. The liberation process includes developing allies—for example, Africans and African descendants build alliances with Indigenous people, white people build alliances with people targeted by racism, and so on.

Listening pair — another name for the Co-Counseling session.

Oppression — the systematic mistreatment of a group of people by the society or by another group of people who serve as agents of the society, with the mistreatment encouraged or enforced by the society and culture.

Oppressor group — the group of people (e.g., white people) that is conditioned to act out oppressive behaviors toward groups the society targets with the oppression (e.g., racism).

Oppressor role — the role of individually enacting some piece of the society's racism (or other oppression).

People targeted by racism — those who are oppressed by racism—for example, African or African descendant, Indigenous, Asian or Asian descendant, Latin American, or Arab or Arab descendant peoples.

Race — pseudo-scientific categorizing of human beings by minor and insignificant physical characteristics such as skin color, facial features, body types, and so on. This categorizing is entirely misleading as our species is one race, the human race.

Racism — the one-way, systematic mistreatment of a group of people on the basis of "racial" characteristics, which is reinforced by society. (We say "racial" in quotes because we believe that while human beings have cultural, social, religious, or other differences, we share many more commonalities than we have differences, and there is only one race of our species, the human race.)

Re-evaluation Counseling — a well-defined practice of listening, taking turns listening, and allowing and assisting emotional release, which enables participants to remove the effects of past hurts and to think clearly where they had previously been confused.

Session — the arrangement in which Co-Counseling takes place—two people divide time equally to listen to one another without interruption and encourage emotional release.

Support group — a group of three to eight people taking equal turns listening to one another and encouraging emotional healing. The group can be based on specific constituencies (African descendants, women, young people, and so on), or issues (educational change, care of the environment, and so on), or it can be a diverse gathering.